F O R

. . . .

F R O M

. . . .

Also see the earlier books

HYMNS FOR A KID'S HEART
Hymns for a Kid's Heart, Volume One
Hymns for a Kid's Heart, Volume Two

GREAT HYMNS OF OUR FAITH
BOOK 1:
O Worship the King

BOOK 2:
O Come, All Ye Faithful

BOOK 3:
What Wondrous Love Is This

BOOK 4:
When Morning Gilds the Skies

FOCUS ON THE FAMILY.

Christmas Carols

— FOR A —

Kid's Heart

Illustrations by Sergio Martinez

Bobbie Wolgemuth
Joni Eareckson Tada

CROSSWAY BOOKS · WHEATON, ILLINOIS · A DIVISION OF GOOD NEWS PUBLISHERS

Published by Crossway Books
A division of Good News Publishers
1300 Crescent Street
Wheaton, Illinois 60187

Design: UDG|DesignWorks, Sisters, Oregon

First printing, 2004

Printed in United States of America

ISBN 1-58134-626-3 Book and CD (sold only as a set)

All music arrangements copyright © by Larry Hall Music

LIBRARY OF CONGRESS CATALOGING-IN-PUBLICATION DATA
Wolgemuth, Bobbie.
Christmas Carols for a kid's heart / Bobbie Wolgemuth, Joni Eareckson Tada; illustrations by Sergio Martinez.
    p. cm.
ISBN 1-58134-626-3 (hc : alk. paper)
1. Carols—History and criticism—Juvenile literature. I. Tada, Joni Eareckson. II. Sergio Martinez, 1937– III. Title.
BV530.W65 2004
264'.23—dc21
                    2004011103

LB   11   10   09   08   07   06   05   04
14   13   12   11   10   9   8   7   6   5   4   3   2   1

To Missy and Julie,

*my favorite memory-makers. I can still see you in footed pajamas
coming down the steps on Christmas morning. And I can still hear your sweet baby voices
singing carols by the lighted tree waiting for Daddy
to read the Bible story. Precious daughters, you are now the mothers of the
next generation of carolers. You light up my life with your joy.*

BOBBIE WOLGEMUTH

To Tom, Mac, David, Ben and Alex Brewbaker...

*May you endure hardship as good soldiers,
keep noble in heart and pure in character, and may you always
belt out these hymns at the top of your lungs.
Thank you for loving Jesus . . . and encouraging me.*

JONI EARECKSON TADA

SPECIAL THANKS TO:

Mr. John Duncan
Executive Producer of the musical recording
for *Christmas Carols for a Kid's Heart.*

Larry Hall, arranger

Mrs. Lynn Hodges, Children's Director

Singers:
Erin Williams
Merrell Pressley
Misha Goetz
Caroline Fisher
Jane Carter
Alex Taylor
Mary Peyton Hodges
Abby Schrader
McDow Duncan

We are deeply grateful for the gifts of these friends and accomplished professionals.

The publisher's share of income from *Christmas Carols for a Kid's Heart* compact disc is being donated by Good News Publishers/Crossway Books to Joni and Friends, the worldwide disability outreach of Joni Eareckson Tada. For more information about Joni and Friends, please write to Joni and Friends, Post Office Box 3333, Agoura Hills, California 91301 or call 818-707-5664 or go to the website—www.joniandfriends.org

Table of Contents

Introduction

Just say the word *Christmas*. It's enough to bring giggles and shivers of anticipation to any child, no matter how old he or she is. Like the fun of trimming the tree with popcorn and homemade decorations collected over the years, it has been our pleasure to pull these treasured carols from our musical collection.

Hot roasted turkey, spicy Christmas puddings, church services aglow in soft candlelight, a brightly lit Christmas tree, children unwrapping presents, cards and photos from friends afar—the traditions may vary, but whatever they are, it's the children who are sure to be the focus of attention. Little wonder our own childhood memories have endured over so many years. Memories of long-ago Christmastimes dust off the childlike delight we yearn to keep alive in our adult hearts. It's a season for family togetherness, for sharing and caring and giving, for keeping alive old traditions and starting new ones. It's a time for quietly focusing on the reason we celebrate the season.

Everyone has a favorite Christmas tradition, and for us, it's the singing of carols. Christmas just isn't, well . . . *Christmas* unless we're happily harmonizing on an old carol, belting out the words at the top of our lungs. The velvety richness of musical notes and the beauty of time-honored words are like presents piled high under the tree. We just can't wait to open them with singing! And there are so many Christmas carols to choose from, we can hardly decide which one to open first.

Christmas carols are timeless. Their beauty and value resist the passing of the years. The warmth of their melodies meld our hearts together with those who may no longer sit around our dinner tables. Or on horseback, as in Joni's case . . .

One snowy night, my parents lined us up at the back door and began dressing us in our coats and scarves. "Daddy, why are we going to the horse stables *now?*" my sister Jay asked. "It's not time to go riding."

"You'll see," my father said, a gleam in his eye.

Our truck rumbled through the quiet streets of town toward the stables. The windshield wipers slapped away wet snow, and the engine whined as our tires slid. It was almost Christmas, and the houses in our neighborhood were covered in blankets of white, with sparkling colored lights lining the eaves, windows, and doors. Within an hour we were back on those same streets— not in the old truck, but on horseback. With thermoses full of hot chocolate in our saddlebags, we guided our horses up and down our street, stopping under every lamppost to sing Christmas carols.

It felt strange to sit on top of my pony and look down on the same sidewalks where I rode my bike during the summer. And it was wonderfully strange to wave to our neighbors as they opened their doors to chime along on "Silent Night." I felt as though the Christmas carol had turned a key in my heart: "Silent night! Holy night! All is calm, all is bright . . ." (from my book *The God I Love*).

The tender story from God's Word comes alive every time we sing these carols. The celebration of the birth of the Christ-Child tunes our childlike hearts to see the brightness of His star.

The Creator of the world chose the music of angels to usher in the first Christmas. And the music of the carols is still introducing us to the best part of the season.

Whatever else might change, the carols we sing at Christmas remain the same throughout the years. They are beloved for that very reason. Carols never date or sound old-fashioned. Instead, they fill our anxious hearts with peace. They bring us joy.

We hope these hymns and the deep meaning of their message become part of your family's Christmas tradition. As you pass them on to the children you love, may you, too, sense the joy of creating a treasured Christmas memory that will warm your hearts for years to come!

All is calm, all is bright.

Joni Eareckson Tada   Bobbie Wolgemuth
Agoura Hills, California   *Orlando, Florida*

The First Christmas

LUKE 2:1-19

In those days a decree[+] went out from Caesar Augustus[+] that all the world should be registered.[+] This was the first registration when Quirinius was governor[+] of Syria. And all went to be registered, each to his own town. And Joseph also went up from Galilee, from the town of Nazareth, to Judea,[+] to the city of David, which is called Bethlehem, because he was of the house and lineage of David,[+] to be registered with Mary, his betrothed,[+] who was with child.[+] And while they were there, the time came for her to give birth. And she gave birth to her firstborn son and wrapped him in swaddling cloths and laid him in a manger, because there was no place for them in the inn.

And in the same region there were shepherds out in the field, keeping watch over their flock by night. And an angel of the Lord appeared to them, and the glory[+] of the Lord shone around them, and they were filled with fear. And the angel said to them, "Fear not, for behold, I bring you good news of a great joy that will be for all the people. For unto you is born this day in the city of David a Savior,[+] who is Christ the Lord. And this will be a sign for you; you will find a baby wrapped in swaddling cloths and lying in a manger." And suddenly there was with the angel a multitude of the heavenly host[+] praising God and saying,

"Glory to God in the highest,
and on earth peace among
those with whom he is pleased!"

When the angels went away from them into heaven, the shepherds said to one another, "Let us go over to Bethlehem and see this thing that has happened, which the Lord has made known to us." And they went with haste[+] and found Mary and Joseph, and the baby lying in a manger. And when they saw it, they made known the saying that had been told them concerning this child. And all who heard it wondered at what the shepherds told them. But Mary treasured up all these things, pondering them in her heart. And the shepherds returned, glorifying[+] and praising God for all they had heard and seen, as it had been told them.

[+]All words marked in this way are defined in the "Do You Know What It Means?" section at the back of this book.

Christmas Carols

For unto you is born this day in the city of David,
a Savior, who is Christ the Lord.

No Ordinary Announcement

TRADITIONAL FRENCH CAROL

*And an angel of the Lord appeared to them, and the glory of the Lord shone
around them, and they were filled with fear. And the angel said to them, "Fear not,
for behold, I bring you good news of a great joy that will be for
all the people. For unto you is born this day in the city of David, a Savior,
who is Christ the Lord. . . . And suddenly there was
with the angel a multitude of the heavenly host. . . ."*

LUKE 2:9-11, 13

Many, many years ago, all the angels in the heavens were called to come before the throne of God for a special event. God wanted to pick one special angel to send on the most important journey ever taken by one of the heavenly hosts. The angel was selected and given instructions, then sent out across the wide expanse of the universe. He flew by spinning planets and soared past twinkling stars. Finally the angel arrived at the edge of a small galaxy. He hovered for a minute and then proceeded past more suns and stars until he arrived on the edge of the atmosphere above one certain planet. That planet was earth. The angel did not pause but continued his flight across continents and oceans until he stopped above a barren land tucked up against mountains on one side and an ocean on the other. It was the little country of Judah.

The night was dark, and the stars gleamed above the angel. He moved breathlessly and quietly until he came to a little village tucked in the hills of Judea.⁺ There below him lay the sleepy town of Bethlehem⁺. It was an ordinary night. Shepherds stood guard over their flocks while the little lambs slept beside their mothers. All was peaceful. All was quiet. But it wouldn't stay quiet for long. This particular angel was an angel of the Lord, and he had been sent by God on a very important mission.

Suddenly the sky opened up. Dazzling light from heaven above streamed upon the hillside. The shepherds almost fell over, for "the glory⁺ of the Lord shone around them." They squinted through the blinding brightness and saw—with shock and amazement—the powerful angel. He had stepped through the thin veil of sky to appear to the shepherds! They dropped to their knees, filled with fear. But the angel of the Lord said, "Fear not, for behold, I bring you good news of a great joy. . . . For unto you is born this day in the city of David a Savior,⁺ who is Christ the Lord."

This was no ordinary announcement. This was a heaven-shaking moment. This was such good news that heaven couldn't contain itself. Before the angel of the Lord could say another word, the night sky burst wide open. The stars faded, and the clouds scattered. Rays of heavenly light shot out in all directions. "And suddenly there was with the angel a multitude of the heavenly host,⁺ praising God and saying, 'Glory⁺ to God in the highest, and on earth peace among those with whom he is pleased.'"

It seemed that angels from all over heaven had turned out for the celebration. Thousands of them lifted their heads, raised their arms, and sang at the top of their lungs. The singing of so many angels vibrated not only the air around the shepherds, but the ground under their feet. The angels' voices shook the earth, rattling rocks and scattering pebbles. The shepherds were breathless. They didn't know whether to cover their ears or run. They stopped and listened closer to the angels' song. They heard the angels say, ". . . on earth peace among those with whom he is pleased." The shepherds turned to each other and smiled. They realized they didn't have to fear these powerful angelic beings. The angels were bringing good news.

The shepherds knew a real king had been born that night—they knew because the birth announcement was delivered by real angels! Suddenly the angel of the Lord and the multitude of other angels vanished. The dazzling light faded, and the sky began to grow dark again. The shepherds looked at one another. Had they really seen what they thought they saw? Had their ears really heard what they thought they heard? Yes, they were certain of what they saw and heard! They quickly ran down the hill to find the place where the new King had been born. The sheep they left on the hill settled back down to sleep. It turned back into an ordinary night.

Or was it? It's not every day an angel crosses many galaxies to give such an important message. There's nothing ordinary about angels talking to men. And it's not every day a king is born. The angels came to announce that the awful trouble between God and people was over. God had come up with a way for people to get close to Him, a way to come back to Him, a way of peace. Jesus was God's peace, and He had been born just moments earlier in a little stable below the hills of Bethlehem.

Even though the angels were now gone and the hills were once again quiet, their song still echoed[+] down the ravines and canyons below Bethlehem. "Gloria in excelsis Deo!"[+] Yes, glory to God in the highest. The Prince of Peace had come to earth! The war between God and man was over.

And *nothing* would ever be ordinary again.

JONI EARECKSON TADA

Angels We Have Heard on High

2. Shepherds, why this jubilee?
   Why your joyous strains prolong?[+]
   Say what may the tidings[+] be,
   Which inspire your heav'nly song?

   Glo - - - - - ria in excelsis Deo,[+]
   Glo - - - - - ria in excelsis Deo!

3. Come to Bethlehem and see
   Him whose birth the angels sing;
   Come, adore on bended knee
   Christ the Lord, the newborn King.

   Glo - - - - - ria in excelsis Deo,
   Glo - - - - - ria in excelsis Deo!

[+] All words marked in this way are defined in the "Do You Know What It Means?" section at the back of this book.

A Verse for My Heart

Are [the angels] not all ministering spirits sent out to serve
for the sake of those who are to inherit salvation?—Hebrews 1:14

A Prayer from My Heart

Dear Lord of all the heavenly hosts, thank You for sending angels
to protect me. I'm so glad that the angels serve You
and obey You too. I want to serve You and obey You too.
Just like the angels! Amen.

Waiting for the Gift

ISAAC WATTS, 1674-1748

GEORGE FREDERICK HANDEL, 1685-1759

And we know that the Son of God has come
and has given us understanding, so that we may know him who is true. . . .
He is the true God and eternal life.

1 JOHN 5:20

Waiting to open a beautifully wrapped gift that has your name on it is a very hard thing to do. Even though you don't know what's inside, you may have been given some hints about the present. You can hardly wait for the day when you get to open this gift.

The people living long ago in the land of Palestine had been waiting a very long time for a special gift. These Jewish people had been praying and longing for the One God had promised to send. God had been giving hints to His people ever since the beginning of the world. He told Eve that someday one of her offspring⁺ would defeat sin and death. This wonderful Child would bring salvation and goodness and everlasting life to people.

Centuries later God promised Abraham that one of his descendants would be the promised Child and that all the nations of the earth would be blessed through His special birth.

God had also been giving hints about the Messiah to be born, through men called prophets. The great prophet Isaiah, who lived about seven hundred years before the Child, said this about the baby: "For to us a child is born, to us a son is given; and the government shall be upon his shoulder, and his name shall be called Wonderful Counselor, Mighty God, Everlasting Father, Prince of Peace." This is written in the book of Isaiah, chapter 9.

Another prophet named Micah had even foretold *where* this wonderful child would be born—in the town of Bethlehem.[+] Yes, God kept sending clues to the people about the promised gift. But it was still not quite time for the gift to be opened.

There was something else God did to get everyone ready for the gift. He sent a baby named John to a very old couple whose names were Zechariah and Elizabeth. They had prayed many years but did not have any children. They thought they were much too old to have a baby, but God wanted to work a miracle. An angel told Zechariah that their baby boy would grow up to tell everyone that the Savior[+] of the world had come to earth.

With all these hints and clues, can you imagine the excitement when the time finally came for the promised child to be born? No wonder every Jewish mother hoped deep in her heart to have a little boy who would be the long-awaited Messiah.

In the city of Nazareth there lived a young girl named Mary, who was Elizabeth's cousin. An angel appeared to her with a surprising message: "Do not be afraid, Mary, for you have found favor with God. And behold, you will conceive in your womb and bear a son, and you shall call his name Jesus. He will be great and will be called the Son of the Most High."

Mary was confused, because she was a virgin and had never slept with a man. She didn't know how she could be a mother without having a husband.

The angel said that God would overshadow her with His Holy Spirit and the child inside her body would be called holy—the Son of God. Mary believed God and sang a magnificent song. Her voice praised God with every note and word. She was overjoyed with the news.

This true story written in the Bible centuries ago inspired two musicians who have given us the Christmas hymn "Joy to the World!" The words of the carol were written by Isaac Watts, and the glorious melody was written by George Frederick Handel. Isaac Watts was the boy who loved to write poems and wrote the hymns "O God, Our Help in Ages Past" and "We're Marching to Zion." He had a way of helping us enjoy great thoughts from the Bible with energetic songs.

You will like the story about George Frederick Handel who also wrote the words and beautiful music to the Christmas oratorio called *The Messiah.* He stayed inside his house for twenty-four days, because God had placed the masterpiece in his head and he was trying to write it down without any interruptions. His friend brought him food, but Handel hardly ate anything. When he wrote the song called "The Hallelujah Chorus," there were tears of joy in Handel's eyes. His heart was full of happiness. Handel said to his friend, "I think I did see all heaven before me and the great God Himself!"

And this man was also bubbling over when he wrote the melody for "Joy to the World," the carol that you sing today.

Are you ready to open the nicest gift? Now that you know some of the hints told in the Bible about the special baby, it is time to receive the gift. You can sing like Mary did when she heard the good news. "My soul magnifies the Lord!"

"Joy to the world! And heaven and nature sing" . . . and all the children too!

BOBBIE WOLGEMUTH

Joy to the World!

2. Joy to the earth! The Savior⁺ reigns: Let men their songs employ;
   While fields and floods, rocks, hills, and plains
   Repeat the sounding joy, repeat the sounding joy, repeat, repeat the sounding joy.

3. No more let sins and sorrows grow, Nor thorns infest the ground;
   He comes to make His blessings flow, Far as the curse is found,⁺
   Far as the curse is found, Far as, far as the curse is found.

4. He rules the world with truth and grace, And makes the nations prove
   The glories of His righteousness, And wonders of His love,
   And wonders of His love, And wonders, wonders of His love.

A Verse for My Heart

Thanks be to God for his inexpressible gift!—2 Corinthians 9:15

A Prayer from My Heart

Father in Heaven, You sent the best Gift to the world! Thank You for
sending hints about the Gift long before You sent Your Son, Jesus. I want to
sing with joy because I have received Your Gift into my heart. Amen.

Messengers of the King

CHARLES WESLEY, 1707-1788

FELIX MENDELSSOHN, 1809-1847

"Behold, I bring you good news
of a great joy that will be for all the people."
LUKE 2:10b

"Hear ye, hear ye!" shouted the king's messenger. From atop his tall, sleek horse he exclaimed, "I have been sent from the palace to proclaim the news to all villagers. The royal decree+ has gone throughout the land that all should know what good tidings+ come from the king's castle. Listen well, fellow citizens, for the heir to the monarch has just been born."

It was the custom in ancient times to send the king's fine soldiers to ride throughout the kingdom and pronounce news from the palace. Trumpets would blow, calling people from their homes to listen to the proclamation. In those days there were no billboards along the highway, no nightly TV news broadcasts, and certainly no computers to tell the latest happenings. The birth of the king's son—the one who would be the *next* king—was news worth shouting about. You can understand why it was the talk of all the people when an heir to the throne had come.

When the King of all kings came to earth, it's no wonder that God sent some messengers to proclaim the news. But whom could God possibly send to announce the birth of His own Son? He dispatched an army of angels from His heavenly throne room to tell the story. Or perhaps I should say, *sing* the story. Yes, God, the Great Monarch of the Universe, sent the proclamation out by way of singing angels. And ever since the first Christmas, people have been singing the story.

Let me tell you about two talented musicians living in Europe who gave us something wonderful to sing at Christmastime. It is one of the finest announcements you will ever hear. One man wrote the words, and the other wrote the music. These special human heralds—messengers— were Charles Wesley and Felix Mendelssohn.

Charles Wesley, who had eighteen brothers and sisters, announced why God's Son was born by writing the words to the carol, "Hark! the Herald Angels Sing." His mother had taught every one of her nineteen children that God had an important job for each of them. In this carol, Charles tells us that God's Child had a very special assignment. He wrote that Jesus made it possible for God and sinners to be reconciled[+]—brought together as friends.

"Hail the heaven-born Prince of Peace!" is what the angels sang that first Christmas night when they proclaimed the royal birth. And that's really good news for you and me.

It's no wonder that the music for this carol makes you so glad, for the man who wrote the tune was named Felix, which in Latin means "happy." And he *was* a very happy musician and successful orchestra conductor because he loved the Bible and listened carefully to God. Although he wrote special anthems for earthly kings, his favorite music to write was praise to Jesus, the King of Heaven. He was a human herald who learned to turn the sounds he heard into noble music to praise God. And what a grand job he did with this carol. It could be called the greatest proclamation of all Christmas songs!

Still today, when something very wonderful happens, an announcement goes out. When you were born, your parents may have sent a card to all their friends telling about your birthday, how much you weighed and how many inches long your tiny little body was. The announcement was probably delivered by the mailman. And unless you have a singing mailman, it was probably just in written form. Can you understand why God would want His announcement delivered by way of mighty, singing messengers? He wanted to include the heavenly hosts because it was such a magnificent celebration.

Would you like to see a herald angel today? It would be fun to hear the voices of those myriads of celestial beings who brilliantly displayed the message of God, wouldn't it? But wait, maybe there is a way to hear God's messengers in a new way. When you sing the story of the newborn King, you *are* a herald. Yes, *you* are one of God's messengers.

And you may be just the one to ride over to your friend's house and proclaim, "Hey, I have great news." You can go Christmas caroling as a happy herald. Go ahead and sing the announcement, "Glory⁺ to the newborn King."

BOBBIE WOLGEMUTH

Hark! the Herald Angels Sing

2. Christ, by highest heav'n adored, Christ, the everlasting Lord!
    Late in time behold Him come, Offspring+ of the Virgin's womb.+
    Veiled in flesh the Godhead see;+ Hail th' incarnate Deity,+
    Pleased as man with men to dwell, Jesus, our Emmanuel.+
    Hark! the herald angels sing, "Glory+ to the newborn King."

3. Hail the heav'n-born Prince of Peace! Hail the Sun of Righteousness!
    Light and life to all He brings, Ris'n with healing in His wings.
    Mild He lays His glory by,+ Born that man no more may die,
    Born to raise the sons of earth, Born to give them second birth.
    Hark! the herald angels sing, "Glory+ to the newborn King."

A Verse for My Heart

Is anyone cheerful? Let him sing praise.—James 5:13b

A Prayer from My Heart

Heavenly Father, thank You for sending the singing announcement
about Your Son. I want to be a happy herald and sing about Your kingdom.
Even though I am small, I want to use my voice
to tell my friends about the Prince of Peace. Amen.

Singing a Lullaby

PHILLIPS BROOKS, 1835-1893

LEWIS H. REDNER, 1830-1908

And Joseph also went up from Galilee, from the town of Nazareth, to Judea,+ to the
city of David, which is called Bethlehem,+ because he was of the house
and lineage of David,+ to be registered+ with Mary, his betrothed,+ who was with child.+
And while they were there, the time came for her to give birth.

LUKE 2:4-6

I love to sing, and my guess is you do too! One of the nicest things about singing is having the chance to sing for others. I realize making music in front of others can make you nervous, but that's why it's special to sing for . . . *babies*. (Babies won't make fun if you sing off-key!)

When I used to play the guitar, I loved singing to my niece, Jayme Kay, when she was a baby. In the evening her mommy would give her a bath, wrap her in a little blanket, and place her in her crib to go to sleep. Sometimes Jayme Kay would fuss. That's when her mommy would ask, "Would you mind singing her a lullaby?" I would gladly get out my guitar, tune the strings, and begin softly strumming—and singing—a song. It was a special lullaby my mother used to sing to me when I was very little. After a few minutes, this same sweet song would gently send Jayme Kay off to sleep.

A lullaby is a song for lulling a baby to sleep. It's a cradle song. Lullabies are very simple songs that are easy to sing. The words are simple too. The messages in a lullaby are always full of comfort. They are peaceful, sweet songs. Lullabies are meant to be sung softly and tenderly.

Lullabies and babies seem to go together. Of all the Christmas hymns we sing, "O Little Town of Bethlehem" is one of the sweetest, loveliest carols. It's easy to think that on the night baby Jesus was born, Mary sang a lullaby to Him. After all, it was dark and cold. The floor of the stable was dirty and damp. Dust from the hay and straw floated in the air. A cool night draft probably sent a chill through Mary. Baby Jesus squirmed in her arms, and she tightened the swaddling cloth around Him. She wanted to comfort her baby and show Him how much she loved Him.

Maybe Mary remembered times when her mother sang to her when she was little. And so as Mary touched the cheek of Jesus, perhaps a lullaby— one that she remembered from her childhood—came to mind, and she tenderly began to sing. I can picture little baby Jesus relaxing in her arms.

I can also picture a few other "babies" being drawn to the lullaby. I'm sure there were many animals in the stable, and some of them could have been little calves or colts or lambs or baby chicks. The baby animals became curious when they heard the beautiful, sweet melody. They were drawn to Mary's soft voice and her lovely song. Taking little baby steps, the lambs edged closer to the manger. They lifted their heads, sniffing the scent of a newborn infant. They were only simple animals, but they, too, wanted to show respect and honor. They cocked their heads and twitched their ears, listening to Mary's song. Like I said, lullabies and babies go together.

Listen to the words of "O Little Town of Bethlehem." *O Little Town of Bethlehem, how still we see thee lie. Above thy deep and dreamless sleep, the silent stars go by; yet in thy dark streets shineth, the everlasting Light; the hopes and fears of all the years are met in thee tonight.*

This lovely, gentle Christmas hymn is a very simple song that is easy to sing. The words are simple too. The message in "O Little Town of Bethlehem" is full of comfort. It is a peaceful, sweet song, meant to be sung softly and tenderly. Yet as simple and sweet as this song—this lullaby—is, its message is *powerful*. Think of it. All the hopes, all the dreams and visions that any one of us could ever have, all the wonder and imagination . . . *all* of it was met that quiet night in Bethlehem. All of it was met in the birth of Jesus, your Savior[+] and mine.

If ever you have trouble getting to sleep, try singing to yourself (you won't have to be embarrassed if you sing off-key!). If ever you toss and turn in bed feeling anxious, sing yourself a lullaby! Memorize the words to this special Christmas hymn. The words are full of comfort, and soon—before you can even count sheep—you will drift off to sleep. You'll sleep as sweetly and soundly as a newborn baby. For you will be reminding yourself of wonderfully comforting things . . . of powerful things: *O holy Child of Bethlehem, descend to us, we pray; cast out our sin and enter in; be born in us today. We hear the Christmas angels the great glad tidings[+] tell; O come to us, abide with us, our Lord Emmanuel.*[+]

Now *that's* a peaceful, comforting lullaby that will chase away any fear or worry in the middle of the night when you can't get to sleep. There's no need to fuss. Just turn over in bed, fluff your pillow, and pray—or rather, sing— "O come to us, abide with us, our Lord Emmanuel."[+]

JONI EARECKSON TADA

O Little Town of Bethlehem

O lit- tle town of Beth- le- hem, how still we see thee lie; a-
bove thy deep and dream- less sleep the si- lent stars go by; yet
in thy dark streets shin- eth the ev- er- last- ing Light; the
hopes and fears of all the years are met in Thee to- night.

2. For Christ is born of Mary; and gathered all above,
   While mortals⁺ sleep, the angels keep their watch⁺ of wond'ring love.
   O morning stars, together proclaim the holy birth!
   And praises sing to God the King, and peace to men on earth.

3. How silently, how silently, the wondrous gift is giv'n!
   So God imparts to human hearts⁺ the blessings of His heav'n.
   No ear may hear His coming, but in this world of sin,
   Where meek souls⁺ will receive Him still, the dear Christ enters in.

4. O holy child of Bethlehem, descend to us,⁺ we pray;
   Cast out our sin and enter in; be born in us today.
   We hear the Christmas angels the great glad tidings⁺ tell;
   O come to us, abide with us, our Lord Emmanuel.⁺

A Verse for My Heart

But you, O Bethlehem Ephrathah, who are too little to be among the clans of Judah, from you shall come forth for me one who is to be ruler in Israel, whose origin is from of old, from ancient days.—Micah 5:2

A Prayer from My Heart

Heavenly Father, thank You for giving us songs in the night.
They comfort me when I'm afraid or I can't get to sleep.
Help me to learn the words to this special Christmas hymn so
I can sing myself to sleep . . . just like a lullaby for a baby! Amen.

Signposts in Heaven

TRADITIONAL ENGLISH CAROL

W. SANDY'S *CHRISTMAS CAROLS*, 1833

Now after Jesus was born in Bethlehem of Judea⁺ in the days
of Herod the king, behold, wise men from the east came to Jerusalem, saying,
"Where is he who has been born king of the Jews? For we saw his star
when it rose and have come to worship him."

MATTHEW 2:1-2

When you look up at the night sky, do you know that you are looking back in time? The light that comes from stars takes so long to reach the earth that the twinkle you see now is what they looked like centuries ago when their light began its journey to the earth.

The stars in the dark sky look small because they are faraway, but they are really quite large. Some stars, like the sun, are huge and shine with a steady light. Gigantic swarms of stars are called galaxies. The galaxy we live in is called the Milky Way, and it contains about 100 billion stars, which is more than we could ever count.

The vastness of the heavens may be overwhelming to us, but God made the stars, and He can count every one. And our galaxy is just a smudge in space—there are billions of galaxies and stars. The Bible says that God not only numbers every star, He also calls each one by name. The Creator of the universe decided that stars were very good signposts to help people find Him. Before He sent His Son, God sent the light of a special star to lead the way.

Years before the first Christmas, there were men in the desert lands of Arabia who looked at the night sky to predict the future. These stargazers were called magi, or magicians. Eastern kings believed in fortune-telling as the way to make decisions. Although they had *heard* about the God of the Jewish people and the miracles He performed, the eastern kings didn't believe in Jehovah God and His ways. They looked to magicians and sorcerers[+] to forecast their future.

God had told His people, the Jews, never to consult with magicians or sorcerers.[+] He told His people to trust Him for everything they needed to know about the future. God said He would direct His children with signs and angels and prophets to let them know what to do and where to go. The magicians and stargazers from the eastern countries were going to find out about the wisdom of Jehovah God through a heavenly miracle.

Night after night the magi were looking for signs in the sky when suddenly they saw the brilliant star of Bethlehem.[+] They were stunned by its brightness and beauty. They knew something magnificent must be happening faraway. Their curiosity was so great that they packed their camels and left on a long trip. They set out to follow the heavenly star and see what it could mean.

Somewhere along the journey something began to stir in the magis' hearts. They excitedly talked about prophecies spoken by Jehovah God to the Jewish people. They remembered hearing about a special star that was to come from the land of the Jews. They continued to follow the bright star until they reached Jerusalem.

In this city they met a wicked king named Herod, who was reigning over the region of Judea.[+] The magi told the king about the star that had led them from afar. They spoke of the Jewish prophecy about a Ruler who was to be born in Bethlehem. They told the cruel king that Someone was coming to shepherd the people of Jehovah God. The travelers told Herod that they were going to follow the star to Bethlehem because they thought the story about the promised Ruler was true.

Cunning King Herod pretended that he wanted to give gifts to the baby. He sent the wise men on their way, saying, "Go and search diligently for the child, and when you have found him, bring me word, that I too may come and worship him." But Herod was trying to trick them, for he was jealous and wanted no other king to take his place. He only wanted the magi to find the baby King in Bethlehem so he could kill Him.

God later sent a warning to the magi, who were seeking the truth. In a dream God instructed them not to return to Herod with the news of the baby's whereabouts.

Pointing like a giant flashlight in front of the travelers, the star led them until it came to rest over a special place. The magi were overjoyed as they entered the house where Mary was playing with baby Jesus. It had been over two years of searching and following the star, but at last the wise men saw the radiance of the boy.

Immediately the magi knew this boy was God's promised Messiah. They fell down and worshiped Him. Unloading the sacks slung over the sides of their dusty camels, they brought in precious gifts. The happy men bowed down and spoke words of adoration and blessing over this marvelous baby as they handed Mary the gifts of gold and spices. They were so overjoyed that they wanted to give their most valuable treasures to Jesus.

As the magi left to return to their country, they were careful not to pass where Herod could find them. By following the star and seeking truth from God, they had become wise. They looked up into the night sky and rejoiced that they knew the Creator of the stars. They had seen the brightest star of all. They said to each other, "Born is the King of Israel!" They knew they would follow this King for the rest of their lives.

BOBBIE WOLGEMUTH

The First Noel

2. They looked up and saw a star Shining in the east, beyond them far;
   And to the earth it gave great light, And so it continued both day and night.
   Noel, Noel, Noel, Noel, Born is the King of Israel.

3. And by the light of that same star, Three wise men came from country far;
   To seek for a king was their intent, And to follow the star wherever it went.
   Noel, Noel, Noel, Noel, Born is the King of Israel.

4. This star drew nigh to the northwest, O'er Bethlehem⁺ it took its rest,
   And there it did both stop and stay, Right over the place where Jesus lay.
   Noel, Noel, Noel, Noel, Born is the King of Israel.

5. Then entered in those wise men three, Full rev'rently upon their knee,
   And offered there in His presence Their gold, and myrrh, and frankincense.⁺
   Noel, Noel, Noel, Noel, Born is the King of Israel.

6. Then let us all with one accord⁺ Sing praises to our heav'nly Lord,
   That hath made heav'n and earth of naught,⁺
   And with His blood⁺ mankind⁺ hath brought.
   Noel, Noel, Noel, Noel, Born is the King of Israel.

A Verse for My Heart

The heavens declare the glory⁺ of God, and the sky above
proclaims his handiwork. Day to day pours out speech, and night
to night reveals knowledge.—Psalm 19:1-2

A Prayer from My Heart

Father in Heaven, when I look at the heavens I see Your majesty.
You created all the stars and call them by name. You made me, and You
know my name. Thank You for telling me how to live
when I ask You for directions. I trust You with all my heart. Amen.

A Humble Bed of Hay

CRADLE SONG

And she gave birth to her firstborn son
and wrapped him in swaddling cloths and laid him in a manger,
because there was no place for them in the inn.

LUKE 2:7

The clouds were low and gray, just like the down of goose feathers. As the snow fell in light, little flakes, the barn almost disappeared in a gray haze. I leaned on my elbow and looked out the window of our farmhouse. My mom and older sisters were busy in the kitchen, cooking dinner. The table was all set for a Christmas Eve feast, and soon our aunts and uncles and cousins would be coming. The farmhouse smelled warm and cozy. Turkey was cooking in the oven. I could smell pumpkin pie. I could hear Christmas carols from the kitchen radio. All my chores were done, and it felt nice to sit on the window seat and stare outside.

Sometime during the late afternoon, I pulled on my jacket and boots. I stuffed a few carrots and an apple in my pockets. I went outside and hiked through the snow to the stable. I felt sorry for the horses and goats in the barn. It was cold and windy, and I was afraid they'd feel lonely. All of us back at the house were going to open Christmas presents that evening, and I didn't want the animals to be left out.

When I got to the barn, I had to push hard to open the door. There was lots of snow piled up. Inside the barn, it was quiet. I recall the sweet smell of hay and the cozy odors of the horses. Someone had fed them that morning, but the horses whinnied when they heard me in their stable. Their mangers were empty. They were hungry, and so I went into the feed room and broke open a small bale of hay. I gave each horse some oats and hay, along with a carrot or an apple.

The horses whinnied with excitement. I watched them crunch their oats, carrots, and hay. I leaned against their stall doors and stared at their mangers. The mangers—or the hay troughs, as we called them—weren't very special. They were only there to hold the hay and feed. The mangers were made of wooden boards nailed together. I looked closer. The horses had even chewed the edges of the boards (I guess they chewed the wood when they were anxious, hoping they would be fed quickly). The mangers weren't very clean. In fact, they were pretty dirty. But they had a purpose—to hold hay so the horses wouldn't eat off the ground.

For some reason, the manger took on a different meaning that afternoon. I had never thought about it before, but the wooden troughs were probably a lot like the manger Jesus was born in. I wondered about that. The manger Jesus was laid in was probably just a few wooden boards nailed together. Maybe it was small—just like our horses' hay troughs. It probably wasn't clean either. Perhaps Joseph had to break a bale of hay to make a good bed in the little manger. And that night in the stable in Bethlehem, the humble[+] manger had a special purpose—it was to cradle the King of kings in a bed of hay. That thought made me feel warm and good inside. I was glad that baby Jesus spent the first Christmas among barn animals, too!

When it began to get dark, I headed back to the house. But not before I whispered, "Thank You, Jesus" as I left the barn.

Something about the peace and quiet of that stable warmed me through and through—almost like sitting by the fire back up at the farmhouse. Maybe it was because I was alone. Or because I took time to think—*really* think—as I watched the horses munch their Christmas goodies. Maybe it was the beautiful feeling of being quiet in a stable rather than the hustle, bustle, and music back up at the farmhouse. Or because I stared at the manger and thought of the "little Lord Jesus, asleep on the hay." Mainly, though, I felt warmed through and through because I prayed a simple prayer—I thanked Jesus.

I can't say exactly why or how, but in some way God spoke to me that cold, snowy, December afternoon. I was able to experience what it must have been like for Joseph, Mary, and baby Jesus—I was filled with the wonderful gift of peace and contentment, sitting among my animal friends in a dirty old barn. I learned a new lesson about humility, for I saw firsthand that God can give His best gifts in a simple, wooden manger.

Even as a little girl, I knew I was making a Christmas memory that would last forever. Maybe you don't live on a farm. When you look outside your window, you might see the backyard of your next-door neighbor. Or you may live in an apartment. Or a trailer. Maybe there are palm trees outside your house. Or sagebrush. You might live with your grandma and granddad. Or you could live in a big city.

Not many kids live near a stable with horses and goats. Imagine what it feels like to be in a barn with the animals when it's cool and quiet, when it's almost nighttime. Picture a manger filled with hay. The next time you feed an animal—giving a horse a carrot or holding out a handful of hay—learn a lesson about humility. If God was happy to have His Son born in a stable, God is happier still to see His Son born in your heart!

JONI EARECKSON TADA

Away in a Manger

2. The cattle are lowing,+ the baby awakes,
   But little Lord Jesus no crying He makes;
   I love Thee, Lord Jesus! Look down from the sky,
   And stay by my cradle till morning is nigh.+

3. Be near me, Lord Jesus, I ask Thee to stay
    Close by me forever, and love me, I pray;
    Bless all the dear children in Thy tender care,
    And fit us for heaven,+ to live with Thee there.

A Verse for My Heart

For the LORD takes pleasure in his people; he adorns the humble+
with salvation. Let the godly exult in glory;+
let them sing for joy on their beds.—Psalm 149:4-5

A Prayer from My Heart

Lord Jesus, help me to learn this Christmas what it means to be humble.
If You could be born in a little manger among barn animals,
then I can be content with simple things too. Help me not to want
a lot of "stuff" this Christmas; instead, I want to be happy with my family
and friends and *whatever* You choose to give. Thank You, Jesus! Amen.

Beautiful Hills and the Glory of God

NAHUM TATE, 1652-1715

And in the same region there were shepherds out in the field,
keeping watch over their flock by night.

LUKE 2:8

Not long ago my friends and I visited the country of Israel. I was so excited! For years I had read in the Bible about places like Jericho and the Jordan River. I couldn't wait to explore the narrow streets in the old city of Jerusalem, and we were looking forward to seeing the villages of Bethany and Bethphage. No wonder we were excited about visiting Israel. It's a land where almost all the stories in the Bible took place!

Look on a map and see if you can find the nation of Israel. When you locate it, you'll be amazed. It's a tiny country with a big sea to the west, surrounded on the east by many countries that aren't friendly. Just like in Bible times, Israel has many enemies, and there is much fighting in the land. The people who live in Israel have to be very careful.

One of the first places I wanted to visit was the little town of Bethlehem.[+] I wanted to see if it was still little! We left our hotel very early and looked on a map. Bethlehem was only a few miles south of Jerusalem. It was a beautiful morning, and we began driving down the road.

Soon we came to a checkpoint with a guardhouse and lots of soldiers. We didn't realize it, but we were about to leave the area governed by Israel and enter a territory called Palestine. This was a dangerous area. We were a little fearful, but we asked God to protect us. After the soldiers questioned us, they let us continue down the road to Bethlehem. I looked around as we drove. The people looked sad, and the area was very poor.

Finally we came over a hill and saw Bethlehem. It was a small town with very narrow roads. We traveled a little further to a church that marked the place where Jesus was born. Nobody really knows the exact spot, but it sure looked like the place a stable would have stood. The church was on a rocky ridge, and behind it there was a lovely valley with gently sloping hills on either side. The hills were a little rocky, and you could see several worn, dirt paths where many sheep had been walking. We could even see a few sheep grazing on the hills. A breeze carried the scent of spring grass. A grove of pine trees behind us whispered in the wind. It was so peaceful, so quiet.

I was amazed to think these were the same hills where shepherds watched their flocks the night Jesus was born—they *had* to be these hills; there were no other ones around. I looked up into the sky and was filled with wonder to be standing on the spot where I would have surely seen angels, had I been a shepherd that night.

Staring at the beautiful scene, we began to sing, "While shepherds watched their flocks by night, all seated on the ground, the angel of the Lord came down, and glory⁺ shone around, and glory shone around." After my friends and I finished singing, we sat there for a long time, listening to the quiet and the breeze in the trees. I was so happy we had come to Bethlehem. I was glad we saw the place where shepherds watched their flocks by night, the night the glory of the Lord shone around.

After a while, we walked back up the hill to the church. That's when we saw the barbed wire, the barriers, and more soldiers. There had been trouble in Bethlehem earlier that week, and the soldiers were there to make sure no fighting broke out. We prayed that God would give us a safe journey back to Jerusalem. As we left Bethlehem, I looked over my shoulder at the sheep still grazing on the distant hills. I prayed, "Lord Jesus, the night you were born here the angels announced 'peace on earth.' I realize the angels meant peace in the hearts of all who trust You. But please, Lord Jesus, bring peace to this land that You love and that we love too."

I don't know why the little country of Israel—and the people who live in it—is a land full of such trouble and war. But the Bible says one day Jesus will come back to Israel. He will bring peace to the country. The warring will be over. At that time, "every knee [will] bow . . . and every tongue confess that Jesus Christ is Lord." Until then, please pray for the peace of Israel.

Pray that one day the angels will, once again, come down. Pray that soon the beautiful hills surrounding Bethlehem will be surrounded by the glory[+] of God.

JONI EARECKSON TADA

While Shepherds Watched Their Flocks

2. "Fear not," said he—for mighty dread,
    Had seized their troubled mind[+]—
    "Glad tidings[+] of great joy I bring
    To you and all mankind, To you and all mankind."[+]

3. "To you, in David's town this day, Is born of David's line,[+]
    The Savior,[+] who is Christ the Lord,
    And this shall be the sign, And this shall be the sign."

4. "The heav'nly babe you shall there find, To human view displayed,
   All meanly wrapped⁺ in swathing bands,⁺
   And in a manger laid, And in a manger laid."

5. Thus spoke the seraph,⁺ and forthwith Appeared a shining throng⁺
   Of angels praising God, who thus Addressed their joyful song,
   Addressed their joyful song.

6. "All glory⁺ be to God on high, And to the earth be peace;
   Good will henceforth,⁺ from heav'n to men,
   Begin and never cease, Begin and never cease!"

A Verse for My Heart

Pray for the peace of Jerusalem! May they be secure who love you! May peace
be within your walls and security within your towers!—Psalm 122:6-8

A Prayer from My Heart

Father God, thank You that You came to earth to give peace
in the hearts of everybody who believes and trusts in You. And now, Lord,
I ask You to bring peace to the land of the Bible.
Help the people stop fighting, and help them to turn to You. Help them
understand the true meaning of Christmas. Open their hearts
so they can know that the Savior was born for them too. Amen.

A Place for Broken Hearts

JOSEPH MOHR, 1792-1848

FRANZ GRUBER, 1787-1863

"And they shall call his name Immanuel"⁺

(which means, God with us).

MATTHEW 1:23

In a small village in the Austrian mountains nearly two centuries ago, there lived a poor young mother named Anna and her baby boy, Joseph Mohr. Sadly, the boy's father did not care about babies or home and had left the family all alone. Joseph's daddy was gone, and nobody knew where he was, except that he had joined the army somewhere faraway.

It was winter in Austria, and the snowy mountain town was frightfully cold. Young Anna was a determined and resourceful mother. She rented a small second-floor apartment near the town church where she knitted warm scarves and mittens to sell and make enough money to feed herself and her baby son. As little Joseph grew, his mother often heard his young voice singing sweetly. Hour after hour as she twisted and knit the yarn, Anna prayed for her son. *Where could Joseph find people to mend his broken heart that longed for a daddy?* She left the prayer at the doorway of heaven day after day.

One day she heard the bells of the nearby church and wondered if under the snowcapped steeple there might be someone who would befriend her young son and teach him more about the music he so loved. Wrapping warm scarves around their necks, Anna and Joseph trudged through the snow to the little stone church.

It was inside the church that Anna and Joseph found the answer to her prayers. The people they met there became their loving family. One very kind man heard Joseph sing and was amazed at his pure voice. The generous man offered to pay for Joseph to go to school and take music lessons.

Joseph was thrilled to be able to go to a fine school and to sing in the church choir. He memorized all the words to every song. No studies seemed too hard, no homework too tiresome. The choirmaster and church leaders were pleased with Joseph. Not only was he working hard, but his enthusiasm was contagious to all the other children.

Secretly wishing his own father could hear him sing, Joseph wondered where his soldier daddy was. Putting aside his longing, however, the young musician continued to sing with a grateful heart. He was glad to sing about his heavenly Father. His mother's prayer was being answered as Joseph's heart was slowly knit together with God's love and the kindness from teachers and friends at church.

Joseph enjoyed beautiful music day after day as he grew up. Just a few years out of his teen years, he had an unusual challenge that could have meant a sad Christmas day for all the children in the St. Nicholas church choir. What Joseph did, however, turned the event into a wonderful legend.

It was just a few days before Christmas, and the children were told that the choir would have to cancel the village festival concert because the church organ was broken. "Why couldn't someone come and repair it?" they asked. A blizzard had left the town snowbound, and the children were told, "No repairman could possibly travel on the icy roads and arrive in time for Christmas." The church organist, Franz Gruber, was troubled. He told Joseph Mohr about the problem and the disappointed children.

Joseph remembered how lonely and silent his home had been before he found music and love at the little church. He could hardly imagine Christmas without music. He went right to his Bible. Reading about baby Jesus who was held tenderly by His mother, Joseph thought about his own mother who used to wrap him with the warm scarves she had knitted. Joseph sat down at his small wooden desk. There he wrote the words for a simple song for the children that would not need an organ. Late into the night Joseph worked on the piece that could be sung the next day with only a guitar. The children would be able to sing on Christmas day after all!

Walking quickly to the church the next morning, he set the paper in front of his friend, Franz Gruber. What a dreamy melody Mr. Gruber composed as he read the beautiful words. In less than one hour the carol was ready. The delighted children sang like angels with the echo[+] of their voices and the sweet guitar chords wafting through the old St. Nicholas chapel. It is no surprise that the adults who were listening liked the song too. It was easy to memorize, and soon it was on the lips of all the villagers. "Silent Night" spread all over the country and around the world like a sweet aroma of heavenly peace.

Joseph Mohr never knew if his own father ever heard the Christmas song he wrote. But he secretly hoped that the words of heavenly peace had reached his daddy wherever he was. He liked to think that somewhere a lonely soldier heard the music and felt the love of Jesus.

We can all be glad that one special boy with a mended heart had the tender music of Christ the Savior[+] to give to the world. Let's learn every verse this Christmas. Let's sing, "All is calm, all is bright" because we have the gift of peace in our hearts.

BOBBIE WOLGEMUTH

Silent Night! Holy Night!

2. Silent night! Holy night! Shepherds quake[+] at the sight!
   Glories stream from heaven afar, Heav'nly hosts sing alleluia;[+]
   Christ, the Savior,[+] is born! Christ, the Savior, is born!

3. Silent night! Holy night! Son of God, love's pure light
   Radiant beams from Thy holy face, With the dawn of redeeming grace,[+]
   Jesus, Lord at Thy birth, Jesus, Lord at Thy birth.

4. Silent night! Holy night! Wondrous star, lend thy light;
   With the angels let us sing Alleluia[+] to our King;
   Christ, the Savior, is born! Christ, the Savior, is born!

A Verse for My Heart

"Peace I leave with you; my peace I give to you.
Not as the world gives do I give to you. Let not your hearts be troubled,
neither let them be afraid."—John 14:27

A Prayer from My Heart

Father in Heaven, thank You for the silent calm You bring
to my heart. There is nothing in all the world that satisfies like Your peace.
I will not be afraid when things go wrong but
will trust in the promises You give in Your Word. Amen.

Nothing to Fear

CECIL F. ALEXANDER, 1818-1895

For unto you is born this day in the
city of David a Savior, who is Christ the Lord.

LUKE 2:11

Imagine with me what the trip to Bethlehem⁺ was like for Mary and Joseph. Days earlier in their hometown of Nazareth, Joseph packed up their donkey and then carefully helped Mary sit on top of the animal. Finally they set out on their journey.

The road from Nazareth to Bethlehem was very long. It was dusty and narrow. Joseph walked slowly, leading Mary atop the donkey across valleys and through many streams. On the last part of the journey, the ground became dry and rocky. The little donkey was surefooted (as most donkeys are from that part of the world). Still, it was rough going. It must have been hard for Mary as she held onto the saddle horn for many miles.

I'm sure Mary was tired. She must have been hurting too. Remember, baby Jesus was still inside her, and her tummy was quite large! Oh, how happy and relieved Mary was when Joseph led the donkey around the last curve in the road. They may have paused on the side of the road to take in the sight. There, lying peacefully in the distance, tucked between the hills under the night sky, was Bethlehem, the royal city of David.

Maybe as they stopped on the edge of the road, people walked around them, leading their camels loaded with supplies. Perhaps Mary took that moment to straighten up in the saddle and rub her sore back. She watched more people pass by. Mary became a little nervous because she knew the overnight lodges in Bethlehem would be crowded. Everyone was going to Bethlehem because of the census[+] of Caesar Augustus.[+]

Finally it was time to move on. Joseph gathered the lead line, *click-clicked* to the donkey, and continued their slow walk down the road.

It was dark, but I think Mary could see—and hear—sheep on the surrounding hills. As she looked over her shoulder, she could probably see the shepherds' camps and the glow from their fires. If the shepherds were singing to their sheep, it perhaps reminded her of King David. David lived in Bethlehem a long, long time ago. When he was a little boy, he tended sheep—and sang to them—on these very hills. Mary would have known all about David. He was famous for all the songs he wrote when he was a shepherd. Surely, Mary would have remembered the most beautiful song he wrote:

> *The LORD is my shepherd, I shall not want.*
> *He makes me lie down in green pastures.*
> *He leads me beside still waters.*
> *He restores my soul.*
> *He leads me in paths of righteousness for his name's sake.*

It's not unusual to think that Mary would have thought of this special Psalm during the last mile of her journey toward Bethlehem. Maybe this Psalm had been a comfort to her when she was a little girl. If so, I think these wonderful verses from the Word of God were a big help to her now!

When they finally arrived in the little village and discovered that there was no room in the inn, maybe she comforted herself, thinking, *The Lord is my shepherd; I shall not want.* Maybe when the innkeeper gruffly said, "There's no room!" she calmed her heart and remembered, *Even though I walk through the valley of the shadow of death, I will fear no evil, for you are with me; your rod and your staff, they comfort me.*

Perhaps when Joseph helped Mary lie down on the bed of straw in the stable, and refreshed her with a drink of water, she whispered, "He makes me lie down in green pastures. He leads me beside still waters." Later in the night, when she heard the Roman soldiers and the sound of horses' hooves on the stone pavement outside the stable, she might have whispered, "You prepare a table before me in the presence of my enemies."

And then, in the middle of the night after she gave birth to Jesus, I wonder if she cradled the Savior[+] of the world in her arms and tenderly repeated, "Surely goodness and mercy shall follow me all the days of my life, and I shall dwell in the house of the Lord forever." As the shepherds came to the stable to see the new King, and as sheep drew close to the manger, I wonder if Mary realized she was holding the Lamb of God in her arms. Did she know her little boy was the Good Shepherd who would one day lay down His life for His sheep?

Yes, Mary may have truly thought of David and his wonderful 23rd Psalm that night in Bethlehem. She may have recalled that Bethlehem was his royal city. And now, this same sleepy little village was "royal" for another reason. It was the birthplace of a new King. As she dozed off that night, holding baby Jesus in her arms, she knew there was no reason to fear.

What things are you afraid of? Do scary thoughts about the future make you feel sad? Remember this beautiful Psalm that King David wrote. Think of him tending sheep when he was a little boy out in the fields beyond Bethlehem. Consider how brave Mary and Joseph were, traveling many miles on a little donkey. If God could take care of David out in the fields at night, and if God could take care of the Holy Family in that dark stable—if He could give them peace and comfort—then He can give you peace and comfort too!

JONI EARECKSON TADA

Once in Royal David's City

Once in roy-al Da- vid's cit- y stood a low-ly cat- tle shed, where a
moth- er laid her ba- by in a man- ger for His bed;
Mar- y was that moth- er mild, Je- sus Christ her lit- tle child.

2. He came down to earth from heaven who is God and Lord of all,
   And His shelter was a stable, and His cradle was a stall:+
   With the poor, and mean, and lowly,+ lived on earth our Savior+ holy.

3. And through all His wondrous childhood He would honor and obey,
   Love and watch the lowly maiden+ in whose gentle arms He lay:
   Christian children all must be mild, obedient, good as He.

4. And our eyes at last shall see Him, through His own redeeming[+] love;
   For that child so dear and gentle is our Lord in heav'n above,
   And He leads His children on to the place where He is gone.[+]

5. Not in that poor lowly stable, with the oxen standing by,
   We shall see Him, but in heaven, set at God's right hand on high;[+]
   When like stars His children crowned all in white[+] shall wait around.

A Verse for My Heart

The LORD is my shepherd, I shall not want.
He makes me lie down in green pastures.
He leads me beside still waters.
He restores my soul.
He leads me in paths of righteousness for his name's sake.—Psalm 23:1-3

A Prayer from My Heart

Dear Jesus, I'm so glad You gave us the 23rd Psalm.
The words are so comforting, and they remind me that You are my Shepherd.
I don't have to be afraid of anything,
and this Psalm reminds me to always trust in You. Amen.

How Great Our Joy!

Do You See It?

GERMAN CAROL

And when the time came for their purification according to the Law of Moses,
they brought him up to Jerusalem to present him to the Lord. . . . Now there was a
man in Jerusalem, whose name was Simeon, and this man was righteous and devout,
waiting for the consolation of Israel, and the Holy Spirit was upon him.

LUKE 2:22, 25

It's Christmastime, and you may be traveling to visit friends and relatives. And you can hardly wait to arrive because you're going to see someone you love. Or maybe you're waiting at home for the door to open and your grandparents or cousins or friends to come for a delightful stay. When they arrive, you may be so happy to see them that you give them hugs before they even get inside the door.

People traveled the very first Christmas too. The first time baby Jesus was bundled up and taken to another city, he was less than a month and a half old. Of course, there were no cars and no car seats in those days; so Mary wrapped him up in soft woven blankets and carried him in her arms. And there was only one seat on which to ride. It was on the back of a little donkey, like the one that had taken Mary to Bethlehem.[+] This time it would only be a short trip to the nearby town of Jerusalem.

Baby Jesus was about to be the center of attention in a ceremony held in the magnificent temple in Jerusalem. And people who did not even know Mary and Joseph were about to tell them some amazing things.

— 71 —

Perhaps your parents took you to church to be dedicated or baptized when you were little. A dedication presentation is a very special day in the life of the child and his parents. It was very important to God that every Jewish boy and girl be dedicated. It pleased Him that babies were marked as belonging to God.

Mary and Joseph traveled with their newborn for just such a ceremony and finally reached the beautiful temple. Holding their baby boy close, they walked through the gates and past the pillars toward the center courtyard where they would present him before the priest.

Everything was going along quite normally, when an old man named Simeon excitedly walked over to Joseph and Mary. He had never seen them before this moment. Simeon was a good man and very close to God.

It wasn't every day that Simeon visited the temple, but early that very day he had awakened, knowing he must be there. He had felt a nudge from the Holy Spirit. God was telling him in his heart that a special baby would soon be in the temple. Simeon didn't hesitate. He went right away to see the baby whom God had promised would be the Messiah.

There were probably other babies in the temple courtyard that day, but none stood out like baby Jesus. He had a radiance about him that caught Simeon's dim eyes. The baby must have been a shining sight, for the old man hurried over to Mary and Joseph and reached for the baby as if he were touching a sunbeam. This was surely God's Son!

Mary and Joseph knew this man was a friend of God by the way he talked and gazed at baby Jesus. The young parents let Simeon hold Jesus in his arms. The light and glory[+] of God lit up the old man's face. All his life Simeon had been praying to see the salvation of God, and here it was wrapped in a blanket in his very own arms!

That was when kind, old Simeon started to say wonderful things about the baby. He lifted up his face toward God in heaven and exclaimed, "My eyes have seen the Savior[+] You have given to the world!" Then he said a special blessing over Mary and Joseph. The young parents stood frozen, marveling at how this man ever found them and knew so much about their baby. He told them some of the same things the angel had said months earlier. "How did he know?" they wondered.

As if the surprise of the old man's blessing wasn't enough, something else wonderful happened. There was a godly old woman who was also in the temple court that day. She was called a prophetess because she had special knowledge from God.

This woman, named Anna, must have seen the same glory shining from the baby that Simeon had seen. Walking toward Mary and Joseph, who were holding six-week-old Jesus, Anna joyfully prayed aloud, "Thank You, God, for this baby! This baby is the hope of all people!"

About that same time, Simeon finally called out, "I can die in peace now that my eyes have seen the glory that God promised, the Light that will shine upon all nations!"

Needless to say, the old man Simeon and the old woman Anna were causing quite a stir at the temple as they drew attention to the young parents with their baby. People were listening and trying to catch a glimpse of the baby who had caused such a commotion.

Mary and Joseph marveled that God was again proving all the things He had told them about Jesus. This was no ordinary baby, and they knew it.

Have you ever been so filled with wonder and delight that you felt like bubbling over? That is just how Mary and Joseph and Simeon and Anna felt that day. And God still works miracles. Jesus can fill your Christmas with more love than you can imagine. It can be the best one ever. How great *your* joy will be!

BOBBIE WOLGEMUTH

How Great Our Joy!

2. There shall be born, so he did say, In Bethlehem a Child today.

   How great our joy! Great our joy! Joy, joy, joy, Joy, joy, joy!

   Praise we the Lord in heav'n on high! Praise we the Lord in heav'n on high!

3. There shall the Child lie in a stall,+ This Child who shall redeem+ us all.

   How great our joy! Great our joy! Joy, joy, joy, Joy, joy, joy!

   Praise we the Lord in heav'n on high! Praise we the Lord in heav'n on high!

4. This gift of God we'll cherish well, That ever joy our hearts shall fill.

   How great our joy! Great our joy! Joy, joy, joy, Joy, joy, joy!

   Praise we the Lord in heav'n on high! Praise we the Lord in heav'n on high!

A Verse for My Heart

"Blessed are the pure in heart, for they shall see God."—Matthew 5:8

A Prayer from My Heart

Father in Heaven, thank You for sending the hope of eternal life
to earth in a baby. I want to hear what You say and see
what You want me to see. Help me to speak to my family and friends
with the joy that You put in my heart. Amen.

Happy Thoughts at Bedtime

ENGLISH CAROL, 18TH CENTURY

ENGLISH MELODY

*And the angel answered him, "I am Gabriel, who stands in
the presence of God, and I was sent to speak to you and to bring you this good news."*

LUKE 1:19

I'm going to tell you a true story about two fine young gentlemen[+] who grew up with a very nice bedtime habit. If you like their idea, you may want to try it some night at your home.

The two boys are brothers, Andrew and Erik, and they are my dear nephews. I learned about their unusual bedtime habit one night when they were little boys, staying at my house because their mom and dad were on a trip. It was bedtime, and the brothers had enjoyed a nice day of playing outside and doing all the fun things boys like to do, like climbing and running and playing with my dog. There were certainly no protests when it was bedtime, and the boys brushed their teeth and slipped into their pajamas like little soldiers.

After we read a story and prayers were said, I left their room saying, "Good night, boys." And I didn't close the door all the way because the boys asked if it could stay open a crack, just as many children want when they go to bed—especially in a place that is not their own home.

Walking down the hall outside their cozy bedroom a few minutes later, I heard something strange. Stepping closer to the door, I was sad to hear one of the boys crying. It was Erik. Andrew was trying with no success to calm his little brother by telling him everything would be okay and that their mom and dad would surely come back to take them home in the morning. If you've ever been homesick, you will understand just how the two boys must have felt that night.

Now, what would you do if you heard a young gentleman crying because he felt all strange and scared? You would want to bring him some comfort, wouldn't you? And that's what I wanted to do. But I wasn't sure just how to go about it that night.

Gently opening the door, I walked over to the edge of the bed. There I stood, wondering what I could possibly say to bring relief to the distressed boy. My heart was reaching for a solution when Andrew gave me the best answer of all.

"Aunt Bobbie," he said, "when we go to bed at night, our mom gives us *happy thoughts* so we can have sweet dreams."

"What a lovely idea," I replied, sitting on the edge of their bed. "Right now, if you help me, we can do just that. Let's think of as many happy thoughts as we can before you fall asleep."

Little Erik was wiping his eyes as we started thinking of some pleasant things. "That was fun to cut up apples and make applesauce with Grandma yesterday." "Didn't you laugh when the puppy licked your face today?" "Wasn't the moon especially beautiful tonight, all full and white?"

There were several more happy thoughts we considered as Andrew and Erik's faces began to change from sad to glad. It didn't take much time for it to happen. For as soon as we started saying the happy thoughts we were able to picture all the wonderful things in our heads, and there was no room for scary pictures or sad thoughts to make us frightened or miserable.

Do you know that God sends happy thoughts to people who are afraid? Reading the Bible you will see that almost every time angels came to people, they said, "Don't be afraid!" Then they would give some good news.

The night Jesus was born, the shepherds who were out on the lonely, dark hillside needed happy thoughts—"glad tidings"⁺ for their minds. The angels knew just the right thing to give them that night. Listen to this verse from Luke 2: "And the angel said to them, 'Fear not, for behold, I bring you good news of a great joy that will be for all the people. For unto you is born this day in the city of David a Savior,⁺ who is Christ the Lord."

That is the happiest thought anyone anywhere could ever give. Just like Erik needed help that night when he was homesick, the angels knew how to calm the frightened shepherds. God had given them strong words of comfort and joy to share.

For hundreds of years choirs have been giving people happy thoughts when they sing Christmas carols. "God Rest You Merry, Gentlemen" is a song filled with happy thoughts. And the best way to keep a happy thought in your head is to sing it, for you will notice that it comes back into your head just when you need it. The words come to the rescue when you are sad or lonely. And the nice thing about singing is that it gives everyone around you something wonderful to think about too.

If you need some sweet dreams tonight when you go to bed, remember the merry gentlemen who taught me the lesson of the happy thoughts. Andrew and Erik would tell you that this carol is a good one to give to any fretful heart. Go ahead and sing out some happy thoughts of comfort and joy!

BOBBIE WOLGEMUTH

God Rest You Merry, Gentlemen

2. From God our heavenly Father, A blessed angel came;
   And unto certain shepherds Brought tidings of the same;
   How that in Bethlehem was born The Son of God by name.
   O tidings[+] of comfort and joy, comfort and joy,
   O tidings of comfort and joy.

3. "Fear not, then," said the angel, "Let nothing you affright;[+]
   This day is born a Savior Of a pure virgin bright,[+]
   To free all those who trust in Him From Satan's pow'r and might."[+]
   O tidings[+] of comfort and joy, comfort and joy,
   O tidings of comfort and joy.

4. The shepherds at those tidings Rejoiced much in mind,
   And left their flocks a-feeding,[+] In tempest, storm,[+] and wind:
   And went to Bethlehem straightway,[+] The Son of God to find.
   O tidings[+] of comfort and joy, comfort and joy,
   O tidings of comfort and joy.

A Verse for My Heart

How beautiful upon the mountains are the feet of him who brings
good news, who publishes peace, who brings good news of happiness . . .
who says . . . "Your God reigns."—Isaiah 52:7

A Prayer from My Heart

Father in Heaven, thank You for sending happy thoughts that change
my heart from sad to glad. I want to listen to Your voice when You tell me
not to be afraid. Thank You for music to sing the good news all day or at
night. I will remember Your good tidings of comfort and great joy. Amen.

Gifts from the Heart

LATIN HYMN ASCRIBED TO JOHN FRANCIS WADE, 1711-1786

Then opening their treasures, they offered him gifts.
MATTHEW 2:11

You can hear it in the music and feel it with every hug. It always happens this time of year—people get excited about giving gifts. The spirit of giving seems to get boys and girls especially excited about the Christmas season. I saw it not long ago when I went into a candy shop to pick up a few things. I found a store clerk who helped stack three boxes of chocolates on my lap (this is Joni writing, and most of you know I'm in a wheelchair and can't use my hands).

When it was time to go, I wheeled up to the checkout counter. The clerk told me that the total for my purchase was $17.89. Because my hands don't work, I had to ask the clerk to go behind my wheelchair, reach into my handbag, find my wallet, then stand next to me and open it up and take out a bunch of dollar bills. I said to her, "If you don't mind counting out the quarters and nickels, I think I have enough change to make the eighty-nine cents."

The clerk was very happy to help me. When she opened up my coin purse and saw that I had *a lot* of pennies, she asked if I would like to use them. I knew it would take her time to count out all the pennies, but no one else was in line behind me, so I said, "Sure, let's use up the pennies!"

So she stood next to me and held open my wallet. She proceeded to dig for pennies and count them out on the counter, "One . . . two . . . three . . . four . . ." and so on. But I had no idea I was being . . . *watched!*

Suddenly a little girl ran up to the counter next to me and—*clink!*—dropped a penny into my change purse. Before I had a chance to react, she dashed back to the card rack where she hid behind her daddy's legs. She peeked out from behind her daddy and gave me a big smile. The clerk and I looked at each other with surprise. We wondered why the little girl gave me a penny.

As the clerk put my boxes of chocolates in a bag, I had time to figure it out. The little girl must have been watching me the whole time from behind the card rack. She must have seen me in my wheelchair. No doubt she saw the clerk dig through my wallet to find enough pennies to pay my bill. That's when I realized the little girl must have thought I was poor and didn't have enough money. Maybe she felt a little sorry for me and wanted to be extra nice.

My first thought was to wheel over to the card rack and tell her that I wasn't poor . . . that I didn't need her penny. But that's when the Holy Spirit whispered and told me not to correct her. So instead I wheeled over to the card rack and said, "I want to thank you very much for helping me!" The child gave me a big smile. Then I said to her, "You have the wonderful quality of Christian compassion, plus you are very generous, and if you don't know what that means, ask your daddy here and he will tell you all about it." Her father gave me a wink.

As I left the store, I praised God for that little girl's giving spirit. And I thanked the Holy Spirit for helping me know what to say—and what not to say. Although I did not need the girl's penny, it was much more important that I encourage her generous spirit rather than correct her and say, "Here's your penny back . . . I'm not poor like you think." If a boy or girl wants to be generous, then I'm happy with that!

That's the message behind "O Come, All Ye Faithful." To be faithful⁺ to God is to be generous and compassionate—just like Jesus! God must have been looking down on the candy store and smiling. He smiles at everything that gives him glory.[+] After all, a child's compassion was encouraged, a father was made proud, a proud person was made humble, a store clerk was amazed, and God received glory for it all. My little friend is *full* of faithfulness. She wasn't afraid; she obeyed her God-inspired instincts and came up and humbly presented her gift.

When you sing "O Come, All Ye Faithful" this season, think of a way you can be generous. Ask God to show you how you can help someone. Show kindness to someone in need—maybe there are people in your neighborhood or in your town who need help; maybe you could show faithfulness to God by giving small gifts to older people in nursing homes. Perhaps you know someone in a wheelchair to whom you can give a gift!

When you go to church this Sunday, give a special gift. Your gift could be as small as a penny, but when you give it with a generous, happy, helping spirit, it's worth millions in God's eyes!

JONI EARECKSON TADA

O Come, All Ye Faithful

2. God of God,[+] Light of Light;[+] Lo, He abhors not the Virgin's womb:[+]
   Very God, begotten, not created;[+]
   O come, let us adore Him, O come, let us adore Him,
   O come, let us adore Him, Christ the Lord.

3. Sing, choirs of angels, sing in exultation,[+] Sing, all ye citizens of heav'n above;
   Glory[+] to God, glory in the highest;
   O come, let us adore Him, O come, let us adore Him,
   O come, let us adore Him, Christ the Lord.

4. Yea, Lord, we greet Thee, born this happy morning;
   Jesus, to Thee be all glory giv'n; Word of the Father, now in flesh appearing;[+]
   O come, let us adore Him, O come, let us adore Him,
   O come, let us adore Him, Christ the Lord.

A Verse for My Heart

A man's gift makes room for him and brings him before the great.
—Proverbs 18:16

A Prayer from My Heart

Lord Jesus, help me to look for ways to help other people in need.
I want to be generous and humble in my giving this Christmas, just like
You were generous and humble when You were born in the stable.
Help me not to draw attention to myself, but guide me
as I point people to You. I love You for being so generous! Amen.

Do You Know What It Means?

Abhors not the virgin's womb: Doesn't avoid having to become human.

Alleluia: Praise to the Lord.

Bethlehem: Ancient town in Judea, Palestine where Jesus was born.

Betrothed: Engaged to be married.

Born to raise the sons of earth: To lift people out of sin and give eternal life.

Caesar Augustus: Emperor of the Roman Empire (27 B.C.-A.D. 14).

Census: Counting the people so they could pay taxes to Rome.

Children crowned all in white shall wait around: Those who surround God's throne.

Citizens of heaven above: People who belong to God regardless of their country.

David's line: Ancient king of Israel who was the ancestor of Jesus.

David's city: Bethlehem, where King David was born.

Decree: A law of the land that everyone must obey.

Deo: God in Latin.

Descend to us: Come down to where we are on earth.

Dread had seized their troubled mind: Fear had taken hold of them.

Echo: The repeating or imitating of a sound.

Emmanuel (Immanuel): The name that means "God with us."

Everlasting Light: Light that lives forever and never goes out.

Exultation: Rejoicing greatly or leaping for joy.

Faithful: Constant and reliable friends who are loyal believers.

Far as the curse is found: God's love can change any evil, wherever sin is hiding.

Fit us for heaven: Prepare us for the eternal place with God.

Flocks a-feeding: Sheep who graze on grassy hillsides.

Gentlemen: Courteous, gracious men or boys with a strong sense of honor.

Glad tidings: Good news.

Gloria in excelsis Deo: Glory be to God on high.

Glorify: To magnify God by praising His name and obeying His commandments.

Glory: The greatness of God's beauty, power, and honor.

God of God: The true God who is above all others.

God rest you merry: God grant you happiness.

God's right hand on high: Place of highest power in heaven where Jesus sits on a throne.

Gold, myrrh, and frankincense: Gifts of minerals and spices brought by the magi.

Good will henceforth: Blessings from now on.

Haste: Hurry.

Herald angels: Those heavenly beings who tell about great and unusual events.

Holy infant: The one and only baby who is divinely God.

House and lineage of David: The family and children born generations later.

Humble, humility: Not proud, lowly.

Imparts to human hearts: God gives to people blessings in their souls.

Incarnate Deity: God with earthly form of human skin on.

Israel: Ancient land of the Jewish people, a land between the Mediterranean Sea and the country of Jordan.

Joyous strains prolong: Happy songs go on and on.

Jubilee: Happy celebration when people's debts were paid and they were set free.

Judea: Ancient region of Palestine that included the city of Jerusalem.

Keep their watch: Stay up and wait until morning.

King of angels: God, who sends angels out to do His will.

Light of Light: God, who formed light and darkness with His words alone.

Lowing: The mooing sound of a cow.

Lowly cattle shed: A rough place where animals were sheltered from the weather.

Made heaven and earth of naught: Creation of the world by God with only His voice.

Maiden: Young girl.

Mankind: People, including men and women and children.

Meanly wrapped: Low-quality clothing or poor baby blankets.

Meek souls: Patient and gentle persons.

Mild He lays His glory by: Jesus came from heaven and didn't demand His power as God.

Morning is nigh: daylight is here.

Mortals: People on earth.

Multitude of the heavenly host: A large group of many, many angels.

Noel: Christmas.

Nothing you affright: Not one thing makes you scared.

Nothing you dismay: Not one thing makes you sad.

Offspring: Children.

One accord: Together with everyone.

Place where He is gone: Heaven, where Jesus went.

Poor, mean, and lowly: Not rich, but ragged and of little value.

Pure virgin bright: A clean girl who has never slept with a man and is radiant.

Quake: Tremble with fear.

Quirinius was governor: Roman leader who collected taxes in Syria.

Reconciled: To win over and make someone a friend again.

Redeeming: To buy back with a payment, to set free.

Redeeming grace: God's payment for our sin when we don't deserve it.

Registered: Counted as a citizen by signing a legal paper with your name on it.

Round yon virgin: Over there is a girl who has never slept with a man.

Royal David's city: The ancient city of Bethlehem, where David was born and grew up.

Satan's power and might: The evil one who tries to produce strong wicked acts.

Savior: One who saves us from the control of the evil one.

Seraph: A heavenly being who surrounds God's throne and has three sets of wings.

Shining throng: Radiant group.

Sinners reconciled: Doomed people who are brought back to God.

Sorcerer: A person who uses witchcraft, black magic, or any evil supernatural power over people.

Stall: A place where animals are kept.

Straightway: Right away.

Swathing bands: Long strips of clean cloth used to wrap or tuck around newborn babies.

Tempest, storm: Raging, fierce weather.

Tidings: News.

Triumph, triumphant: Success and victory.

Veiled in flesh the Godhead see: God hidden in the human body of Jesus.

Very God, begotten, not created: Jesus, who existed with God from the beginning.

Virgin's womb: A pure place inside Mary's body where God placed Jesus to grow.

When we were gone astray: Before we admitted we were sinners who were faraway from God.

Word of the Father, late in flesh appearing: Jesus, who already existed before He was put into a human body of a baby.

With His blood: Christ gave His life on the cross to save people.

With child: Pregnant.

My Personal Notes

My Personal Notes

My Personal Notes

My Personal Notes

Welcome to the Family!

Whether you received this book as a gift, borrowed it, or purchased it yourself, we're glad you read it. It's just one of the many helpful, insightful and encouraging resources produced by Focus on the Family.

In fact, that's what Focus on the Family is all about—providing inspiration, information and biblically based advice to people in all stages of life.

It began in 1977 with the vision of one man, Dr. James Dobson, a licensed psychologist and author of 18 best-selling books on marriage, parenting, and family. Alarmed by the societal, political, and economic pressures that were threatening the existence of the American family, Dr. Dobson founded Focus on the Family with one employee and a once-a-week radio broadcast aired on only 36 stations.

Now an international organization, the ministry is dedicated to preserving Judeo-Christian values and strengthening and encouraging families through the life-changing message of Jesus Christ. Focus ministries reach families worldwide through 10 separate radio broadcasts, two television news inserts, 13 publications, 18 Web sites, and a steady series of books and award-winning films and videos for people of all ages and interests.

•   •   •

For more information about the ministry, or if we can be of help to your family, simply write to Focus on the Family, Colorado Springs, CO 80995 or call 1-800-A-FAMILY (1-800-232-6459). Friends in Canada may write Focus on the Family, P.O. Box 9800, Stn. Terminal, Vancouver, B.C. V6B 4G3 or call 1-800-661-9800. Visit our Web site—www.family.org—to learn more about Focus on the Family or to find out if there is an associate office in your country.

We'd love to hear from you!